KORN/FERRY INTERNATIONAL
powered by LOMINGER

Becoming an
Agile
Leader

Know what to do…
when you don't know what to do

Victoria V. Swisher

Becoming an Agile Leader

Know what to do...
when you don't know what to do

Tel. +1 952-345-3610
Tel. +1 877-345-3610 (US/Canada)
Fax. +1 952-345-3601
www.kornferry.com
www.lominger.com

ISBN 978-1-933578-43-9

Item number 82153

1st Printing April 2012
2nd Printing October 2012

Table of Contents

Introduction

Recently, the retired CEO of a multinational chemicals manufacturing company attended a reception in his honor. While making the rounds, he made a point of being introduced to current leaders and asking them about their roles. After one business unit head described his job, the retired CEO declared with some surprise, "That used to be my job as CEO!"

At this company and so many others like it, jobs are progressively getting bigger and more complex, not just for CEOs but all the way through the ranks. And there's no sign of a leveling off on the horizon. It's no wonder, then, that finding or being the "perfect" candidate to match a job profile is becoming harder, if not impossible, to do. More now than ever, even with the best hires, some skills need to be learned on the job.

As you look out over the global work landscape, it seems pretty obvious that the era of job stability and predictability is over. What has become the norm is the need to acquire new skills—all the time. Skills to equip you for a current and future reality where markets, competition, technology, legislation, and business strategies evolve in equal measure organically and disruptively.

Making this situation even more concerning is the fact that while jobs are getting bigger, the supply of qualified people, or talent, to fill jobs is actually shrinking. The population in developed countries has leveled off [1] and, while population in developing countries is exploding, supply of skilled talent isn't keeping pace with those developing countries' sprinting economies.

These factors have contributed to the phenomenon of younger people getting jobs with greater responsibility and greater complexity earlier than ever in the past. Nowhere is this more evident than at the executive level. For example, in 2010, the average age of departing CEOs in the Standard & Poors 500 was 61. These executives had an average tenure of eight years at the time of their departure.[2] That same study found the average age of the *incoming* CEOs of the same group to be 51. What does this mean? If typical CEOs retire at age 61 after eight years in position, their successors should be an average age of 53 coming in, not 51. Now would-be CEOs need to be ready an average of two years sooner than in the past and will likely be stepping into a role more complex than their predecessors held.

Simply put, we're not getting enough time on the job to build the more complex skills, particularly those related to strategy and being effective working with and through others.[3] This skill gap becomes especially problematic in leadership roles. And there's no sign of the gap closing. What's more likely is that no matter what your particular role, you will eventually face new situations, assignments, or challenges that could stump you if you're not prepared.

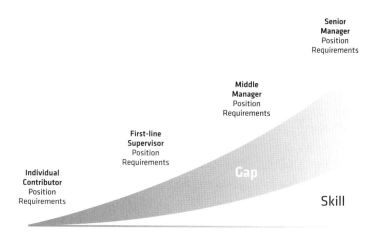

What Do You Do
When You Don't Know What to Do?

So how do you fill the gap? How can you arm yourself so that you successfully tackle those new, unfamiliar situations that are bound to come your way? Through learning. And not just any learning, but learning from your experiences. How? By reflecting and harvesting meaning, or lessons, from each experience you have. By making sense of them and distilling them down to rules of thumb or principles. When you are faced with new and possibly tough situations, those lessons manifest as varied approaches, ideas, solutions, techniques—a treasure trove of options for you to choose from, depending on what the particular challenge calls for.

There is a name for this ability to learn from experience in a consistent, systematic way and then apply that learning in new situations. It's called *Learning Agility.*

Today, and possibly even more so in the future, it will be unlikely that you can walk into a role knowing it all. This is where Learning Agility can make a difference. It's not so much what you have accomplished in the past, but what you will be able to do in the future when faced with a new challenge that will require new behaviors and attitudes or, at minimum, adapting to fit the new situation.

Learning Agility is much more than just an abstract concept. It is characterized by certain behaviors and preferences—both in how we go about our work and the choices we make on and off the job. Because it's a set of behaviors, you can detect Learning Agility in action. And not only can you start to spot these behaviors, you can also choose to develop these qualities in yourself and help build them in others.

Read on and you'll discover how the qualities of Learning Agility come to life in leaders like Richard Branson, Nelson Mandela, and Mary Kay Ash, to name a few. And how *you* can start to build the qualities of agile learning and recognize it in those around you.

To help get you started, here's how the book is organized:

The first chapter, "Learning Agility Unveiled," explores what it means to be an agile learner, the risks of sticking solely with the familiar, and how an agile learning orientation compares to being more focused on mastery or deep expertise.

The remainder of the book is organized around the five key elements, or factors, of Learning Agility: Self-Awareness, Mental Agility, People Agility, Change Agility, and Results Agility. The ordering of these chapters is purposeful. We begin with Self-Awareness because it is becoming clear in the research literature that for any meaningful or long-lasting change to occur, development must begin with a solid understanding of yourself.[4]

Each Learning Agility factor chapter is divided into two sections. The chapters begin with a portrait of a well-known person whose life parallels the traits and behaviors of that particular agility. The first section goes on to describe what the agility is all about, why it matters, and how you can see it in yourself or others.

The second section of each Learning Agility factor chapter focuses on how you can sharpen each agility, including tips that you can take action on now, what may be getting in your way, some on- and off-the-job roles to build and practice, dangers of overusing an agility, and suggested readings to further explore the agility.

We trust you will find value in gaining a clearer understanding of what it means to be learning agile and how, depending on your career and life aspirations, Learning Agility can help you achieve what you're looking for.

The ability and willingness
to learn from experience, and
subsequently apply that learning to
perform successfully under new
or first-time conditions

Learning Agility Unveiled

"Every day I'm learning something new."

Sir Richard Branson – Founder, Virgin Group

How Do You Know What to Do When You Don't Know What to Do?

"My biggest motivation? Just to keep challenging myself. I see life almost like one long university education that I never had—every day I'm learning something new." These words were said by Sir Richard Branson, entrepreneur and owner of Virgin Group.

From the early days of his storied life and career, Richard Branson has been on a quest—a quest to learn. To learn new things, different things, things that challenge him. His entrepreneurial career path has been the opposite of linear. Virgin was initially born from an alternative music magazine, but from there the company, driven by Branson's curiosity and zeal to take on the unfamiliar, has followed a growth course that is anything but ordinary—from recording company, to retail music stores, then a leap to airlines, rail, telecommunications, banking, even space travel.

Branson's decision to start Virgin Atlantic Airways illustrates his drive to explore, experiment, and as he puts it, "create new things." Virgin Atlantic was not conceived from an intense vetting process of poring over business scenarios and financial models, but from a burst of inspiration from Branson.[5] After a particularly frustrating incident when he waited on hold for hours for an airline customer service representative to help him, Branson decided he could do a better job of this himself. Of all the challenges he had taken on, this was arguably the riskiest and farthest from his comfort zone. But he did it. As with all his ventures, there were stumbles, setbacks, and failed attempts, but today Virgin Airlines is a force to be reckoned with in the airline industry.

An avid reader, Branson considers his education to be "an education of life."[6] By his own account, he's "gotten involved with a lot of different things" which has allowed him to expand his perspective, stretch himself, and grow as a result. Branson continues to amass learnings and lessons from his experiences that help equip him as he continues his journey. No one today is really surprised when Branson announces his latest venture or idea—he's made a brand out of pushing himself and Virgin to places that may seem hard to conceive of but that he somehow makes into a reality.

Learning something new. Pushing himself. Looking at things differently. Deliberately seeking out the unfamiliar and figuring out how to get things done when the challenge is new. These qualities in Richard Branson and others like him are found in a particular kind of learner—an agile learner. And with the world around us becoming increasingly complex it seems with each passing day, agility as a learner can make a big difference. Knowing or figuring out what to do in new, challenging situations when you don't, at first, know what to do can help equip you for the change and complexity that is likely to come your way in your career and in life.

Why Not Stick with What You Know?

It's tempting really. Especially if what you know has never steered you wrong before. The reason so many of us fall back on our favorite solutions is we've had a lot of success with them in the past. But as the future becomes increasingly complex, chances are you will eventually face a situation where your tried-and-true solutions and decision rationales may fall short.

Take the case of Dick Fuld, long-time CEO of Lehman Brothers before its collapse as part of the financial meltdown in 2008.[7] Fuld had a single-minded objective—to keep the company independent. And he had a successful precedent to work from. He had steered the 100-plus-year-old company through a previous storm 10 years earlier when a giant hedge fund, Long-Term Capital Management, went under. In that case, Fuld was able to renegotiate loans and secure new capital to ride out the storm. So he figured his successful strategy from that past situation would work again in 2008. Fuld applied what he looked at as proven solutions to a situation that, it turned out, didn't have the same characteristics. His experience riding out the storm of the Long-Term Capital Management crisis didn't prepare him for the financial tsunami of 2008.

Dick Fuld is a very smart man. A very experienced man in his field. But in this instance, perhaps in part due to the allure of quickly resolving the crisis, he may have relied too heavily on past solutions rather than looking at the issue with a fresh perspective.

Overreliance on past solutions—when not balanced with a steady injection of new lessons that yield new ways of doing things—can sometimes lead to career derailment (when a career, successful for many years, goes into eclipse). The leadership research on derailment[8] shows a leading indicator to be the extent to which a person does or does not continuously learn—learn *new* things instead of adding ammunition to support what they already know. In worst-case scenarios, these people had quit learning altogether, were convinced they could do no wrong. As a result, they couldn't make transitions to a different job or adapt quickly to the unfamiliar. They relied on what had gotten them to where they were, ironically becoming victimized by their past successes.[8] Faced with new demands, they got stuck, underestimated the newness of the demands and, instead, assumed the new demands were just another version of what they'd done before.[9]

The same research that delved into career derailment also explored the characteristics that relate to career success.

Those with Successful Careers	**Those Whose Careers Stall or Derail**
Have roughly twice the variety (but sometimes the same number) of on-the-job challenges	Tend to have the same types of assignments but virtually no pattern of learning new things from them; almost seem to have quit learning
Seek and get more feedback on how they come across to others and what they need to do to improve	Have low self-awareness—an imbalanced view of their strengths and weaknesses
Have zigzag careers—with many firsts and some failures	Don't have a clear view of what they aren't good at, so don't think to develop new skills...until it's too late
Respond to this newness and adversity by learning new skills and ways of thinking	Fail when making transitions from the known to the unknown

All this does not mean you should discount your experience and abandon what's worked for you before. It also doesn't mean you won't continue to see success in similar situations. You should both honor your experiences and retain a healthy dose of skepticism about them. When you're faced with a new or tough problem or issue that needs solving, pause before defaulting to what's been the tried-and-true path for you in the past. If the solution or course of action feels comfortable—that's a red flag. If it seems like a winner on the surface—another red flag. Remember that your favored solutions likely have a shelf life. You are bound to encounter new contexts. Different people. Unfamiliar problems. And, eventually, you will come up against a situation where your favored solutions or skills just won't get the job done.

Another way to look at it: Imagine two people standing in front of you. Both have a reputation for doing well and performing. A crisis hits. One of these people is carrying a bag with about ten different strategies and approaches he or she has used in the past. The other person carries a bag with a thousand different strategies and approaches to draw upon. Which person would you follow?

Being an agile learner, or possessing a high degree of what is known as *Learning Agility*, helps you add those strategies and approaches to your own arsenal. Why? Because agile learners embrace new challenges, look at tough problems from broad angles, and readily change to meet shifting demands.[10] Most of all, agile learners—those with high Learning Agility—reflect. They wrest meaning from experience and turn that meaning into principles or rules of thumb they can use going forward.

What Is Learning Agility?

Learning Agility is defined as *the willingness and ability to learn from experience, and subsequently apply that learning to perform successfully under new or first-time conditions*. Its roots are in leadership research as opposed to educational psychology.

This definition of Learning Agility is not meant to imply that if you're not highly learning agile, you're incapable of learning. Everybody can learn. One of the greatest differentiators of the human condition is the ability to learn. When talking about agile learning or being learning agile, it is a particular type of learning that is different from the kind of learning that helps with things like memory, analysis, and comprehending new information. This kind of learning can be termed traditional learning.

It's important not to think of these types of learning in terms of either/or. Everyone has a measure of both traditional and agile learning attributes to varying degrees. What is helpful here is to start to distinguish between the two.

Traditional Learning	Agile Learning
Intelligence, IQ	Quick thinkers
Grades or academic marks, grade point average, class rank	Take initiative
Scores on standardized tests that are used for post-secondary education admissions	Curious—always asking "why" and "how"
	Make fresh connections
	Acquire and use rules and principles
Functional/technical skills	Broad thinkers
Verbal skills	Know personal strengths and weaknesses
Data crunching/ analytical skills	
Straightforward problem solving	

As you can see, Learning Agility is more than intelligence or simply being book smart.[11,12] Learning new job and technical knowledge is different from learning new personal behaviors or ways of viewing events and problems. Street smarts, common sense, or simply learning from life experience is different from how intelligent you are (as measured by IQ tests, grades in school, or accumulating technical knowledge).[12]

Both traditional and agile learning are important—both are needed for success. However, much of what is often praised today,[13] especially in the work world, falls in the traditional learning category. And too much emphasis on traditional learning can be risky.

Several years ago, a large employer of accountants in the U.S. held regular recruiting programs at top-rated university campuses. They recruited about 400 bright, seemingly well-qualified accountants each year. When they conducted a periodic audit of their process, they were surprised to find about a 50% attrition, or turnover, rate from their campus recruits.

This was an expensive proposition for them, so they did a study: were there flaws in their recruiting process that caused such high attrition? It turned out they were hiring solely based on traditional learning criteria—things like grade point average, test scores, academic awards. And with the complex and changing landscape of work in the company, this simply wasn't enough.

So they changed it up a little. Instead of just looking at grades and test scores, they started asking questions to gauge curiosity and an interest in learning a lot of new things. Agile learning characteristics. For example, the recruiters found that the amount and variety of extracurricular activities candidates engaged in was one measuring stick to tease this out. And they stopped automatically passing over the candidates who didn't necessarily have the best grades, since a unifocus on class work isn't a typical trait of agile learners.

The result? A significantly higher two-year success rate for the recruited candidates after implementing the new, expanded criteria.

Having high Learning Agility especially comes into play with transitions—from the known to the unknown. When you face a novel, unfamiliar situation, your existing routines and behaviors may be inadequate. Learning Agility gives you the flexibility to learn new ways of coping with unforeseen problems and opportunities.[14,15] Those who are highly learning agile gain their lessons closer to the event or interaction itself. Not because they are smarter (from an IQ sense), but because they have amassed more learnings from past experiences which helps them figure out what to do when they don't know what to do.

Learning Agility is not binary—where you've either got it or you don't. Like height and weight, it is normally distributed across the general population. So everyone has learning agile tendencies to a certain extent. For the sake of illustrating what Learning Agility looks like, the focus of the descriptions will be on the characteristics of the highly learning agile.

Knowing It When You See It

So at this point you may be wondering, "How do I know if I have high Learning Agility? How do I spot it in others?" The good news is that Learning Agility is a composition of behaviors or competencies. Since Learning Agility is behavior-based, you can observe it in others and begin to recognize the characteristics in yourself. And, importantly, because Learning Agility is a set of behaviors, it can be developed.[16]

To help bring it to life, think about agile learners as excelling in some combination of five areas, or Learning Agility factors.[17]

Throughout the book, we will explore these Learning Agility factors in greater detail and offer strategies to hone your skills in each area.

Learning Agility Factors

Self-Awareness

They know what they're good at and
not so good at and actively address
the not so good

Mental Agility

They are critical thinkers who are
comfortable with complexity, examine
problems carefully, and make fresh connections
that they make understandable to others

People Agility

They understand the value of getting things
done through others and are exceptional
communicators who see conflict as an
opportunity rather than a problem

Change Agility

They like to experiment and can deal
with the discomfort of change; they have
a passion for ideas and are highly interested
in continuous improvement

Results Agility

They deliver results in first-time situations
through resourcefulness and having a
significant presence that inspires others

Mastery or Learning Agility:
Going Deep Versus Going Broad

One of the hallmarks of agile learners is their restlessness. Their curiosity and their eagerness to explore the new and to seek out different experiences keep them searching for the next challenge. It's not surprising, then, that such characteristics run counter to sticking with any one discipline or specialty for long periods.

So not every setting, work or otherwise, is tailor-made for agile learners, nor should it be. Indeed, there are some jobs where being highly learning agile could actually be a detriment and where deep expertise and specialization is the absolute best choice.

This viewpoint would likely be shared by the 155 people on board the January 15, 2009, US Airways Flight 1549 out of New York's LaGuardia Airport. Pilot Chesley Sullenberger, or "Sully" as he is commonly known, was able to accomplish the highly improbable—after both jet engines died when the plane collided with a flock of birds, Sully glided the jet safely into the Hudson River. All passengers and crew were rescued with little to no injuries.

How was he able to accomplish this amazing feat? At the time, Sully was a 29-year veteran pilot with US Airways.[18] His 19,000 hours of logged flight time was almost double the threshold for achieving mastery that Malcolm Gladwell details in his book *Outliers*.[19] Sully had served as a flight instructor and safety chairman for the Air Line Pilots Association. In addition, he had investigated aviation accidents for the Air Force and the National Transportation Safety Board and helped develop new protocols for airline safety. People describe Sully as "the consummate pilot," and the mayor of New York City praised Sully for a "masterful job."

Sully's mastery saved more than a hundred lives that day. In that moment of crisis, it wasn't time to experiment broadly—it was time to access the narrow, deep, focused expertise he had in his field and bring it quickly to the surface.

Where Sully and others like him excel as masters at their chosen craft, agile learners, in contrast, gravitate to careers and life paths that offer variety and breadth. Their curiosity and drive for seeking new challenges lead them to become versed (though typically not deep experts) in not just one or more related disciplines, but in multiple, sometimes very diverse, areas.

Here are some characteristics of people with a high mastery orientation. See how these characteristics compare to those of people with a Learning Agility orientation. Remember that it's likely you will have a mix of both characteristics. Where might you best fit?

Captain Chesley "Sully" Sullenberger

High Mastery (Depth)

Recognized functional, technical, managerial experts

Know current job extremely well so can be counted on, especially in tough times

Superior performers year after year*

Work independently with little or no supervision

Love what they do, may not aspire to broader management

Have depth of organizational knowledge

Excellent at developing people

Trusted resources within the organization

Difficult to replace in kind

Widely recognized outside the company

High Learning Agility (Breadth)

Easily learn new functions

Clever problem solvers

Think strategically

Perform well under new, tough conditions*

Change behavior or approach easily

Have wide interests (highly curious)

Deal well with ambiguity/complexity

Promotable outside their areas, especially into general management and senior leader roles

Like to try different approaches

Impatient, don't accept the status quo

*It's important to note that the one common denominator between those with a mastery orientation and those with a learning agile orientation is that both are considered consistently high performers in their given context.

You can also consider these distinctive qualities when thinking of the types of jobs or assignments each would be best suited for:

If the job or assignment...

Is new

Requires fresh ideas, new ways of thinking

Is in a quick-changing field, area of business where future is undefined or emerging

Needs major fixing

Requires strategic thinking, strategy development

Is supported by strong technical help

Requires political savvy

Is change-driven

...then someone with high Learning Agility would likely be the best fit.

If the job or assignment...

Requires considerable experience in field,
depth of knowledge

Is relatively stable

Requires deep understanding of the past in
order to address future situations

Needs strong and decisive tactical skills

Involves major development/mentoring of others

Is relationship-driven or depends on continuity

...then someone with a mastery orientation
would likely be the best fit.

There is still much to be explored and written on the topic of mastery orientation. We touch on it here briefly for two reasons: (1) to establish clear distinctions between types of high performers, and (2) to illustrate that while possessing high Learning Agility is in many cases beneficial, building a deep expertise can also be of great value.

Much of what is described here comes down to fit—fit between what your learning preferences are and what you want from your career or life experiences. Because Learning Agility can be developed, if you aspire to the kinds of jobs or the characteristics of agile learners, you can choose to focus on growing and practicing those behaviors.

Here's what is known for certain:

Learning from diverse experiences is very beneficial in most situations, especially leadership roles

Dependence on favorite past solutions is risky

With jobs getting bigger all the time, the ability to figure out what to do when you don't know what to do will be critical

Learning Agility is an insurance policy for an uncertain future

As you approach the remaining chapters, think about which description below may apply most to you and use it as a guide to help you determine where to focus. Keep in mind that it's not just where you see yourself today, but how that fits with what you aspire to be, especially in your career.

I see myself as an agile learner in some ways but not in other ways

Read more about the Learning Agility factors to see what fits, what doesn't fit, and what might help you grow

I consider myself to be a very agile learner

Check your assumptions by reading through the portraits of well-known people in each of the Learning Agility factor chapters; also pay special attention to the "Be Mindful Not to Overuse..." sections

I think of myself today as more of an expert with deep, specialized skills

Read through the Learning Agility factor behaviors which may provide useful insight into the traits and characteristics of you or people you know

The degree to which an individual has personal insight, clearly understands their own strengths and weaknesses, is free of blind spots, and uses this knowledge to perform effectively

Self-Awareness

"When you know better you do better."

Maya Angelou – American poet, author, civil rights activist

How Do We Begin to Know Better?

Maya Angelou. Poet, memoirist, novelist, educator, dramatist, producer, performing artist, historian, filmmaker, civil rights activist. And the list goes on. Dr. Angelou's achievements and accolades are frankly too plentiful to list here. She has played many roles in her celebrated life. But what is the common thread that defines them? What quality in Maya Angelou created this fertile ground for achievement?

While Angelou is celebrated for the diversity of her talents and successes, she is also well known for the extent to which she reflects—reflects on her life, her experiences, her stumbles, her triumphs, her strengths, and her weaknesses. Author of six autobiographies (six!), hers is a life examined, to be sure. Yet this introspection has never been without purpose. It has been inward reflection paired with the focus on moving *toward* something—a goal, an aspiration, a challenge—that defines Self-Awareness for Angelou and others like her.

A journal keeper from as early as the age of nine, reflection has been a constant in Angelou's life. But she hasn't just kept the lens turned inward. Part of the equation for knowing yourself is gauging yourself in relation to others—how you are perceived, how you are coming across, what others think of the work that you do. Maya Angelou gets this. She gets that her every word and action reflects on her. One of her more famous quotes speaks to this: "I've learned that people will forget what you said, people will forget what you did, but people will never forget how you made them feel."

Angelou has relied on direct and indirect feedback to help her learn more about herself in service of achieving her goals. Now an accomplished writer, Angelou's first public foray was less than stellar. After reciting her one-act play to the Harlem Writers Guild, she faced some harsh criticism. Angelou realized that if she was going to pursue her goal of becoming a writer, she would have to learn technique and, as she put it, "surrender my ignorance." The feedback from the Guild was a catalyst that set her on the path to achieving that goal.

Gaining personal insights for a purpose. This is the hallmark of Self-Awareness. And this is what Maya Angelou exemplifies. And it is a journey. To this day, Angelou remains realistic about her own gifts. She once was asked in an interview if she considered herself to be wise. Her response? "Well, I'm en route. I am certainly on the road."

Why Self-Awareness Matters

"Know thyself." Socrates' famous quote certainly has merit but may leave you with lingering questions like "How?" "To what end?" Fortunately, Self-Awareness, as we explore it here, is all about practicality. And that by gaining understanding of your strengths and weaknesses (and we all have some of each), you can move toward your goals with eyes wide open.

The research around the benefits of Self-Awareness is pretty clear. In one study, the best predictor of a high performance appraisal was seeing yourself as others see you; the best predictor of a low appraisal was overrating your skills. Deploying yourself against life and work is greatly helped by really knowing what you're good, average, and bad at, what you're untested in, and what you overdo or overuse.

The risk of remaining unaware is that you accumulate blind spots—things you think you're great at but others don't share your view. Known weaknesses can be tackled directly if you choose. A blind spot, on the other hand, is nearly impossible to address because it's a weakness you don't know exists or are unwilling to admit you're not good at it. This leads you to confidently strut into areas that should make you cautious and humble. And disaster can soon follow.

Think of building Self-Awareness as habit-forming. First comes feedback. Feedback you seek out and welcome, whether positive or negative. Then comes internal reflection—making sense of the feedback and distilling it down to rules of thumb you can use going forward. Armed with this new insight, you can begin to bridge the gap between where you are today and what you aspire to, what your goal is. This cycle of gauging perceptions, reflecting inwardly, and then rechanneling can become self-perpetuating. And when it does, you're likely to find that more roads to continue the journey will open up before you.

If you are on the higher end of the Self-Awareness continuum

You are likely to...

Know what you're good at and not so good at

Seldom be surprised by others' feedback

Willingly admit and take accountability for mistakes

View criticism as helpful

Know what causes your feelings and moods

Be candid about your strengths and weaknesses

Solicit and welcome feedback

Gain insights from missteps

And you may say things like...

"I've been reflecting on how
I might have handled that
situation differently..."

"I'd love to get your
perspective on how I came
across in that meeting..."

"This continues to be a problem
area for me. If I'm going to
reach my goal, I need to
keep working on..."

If you demonstrate
Self-Awareness less often

You may...

Be satisfied with who you are

Like to focus on the present—the here and now

Value people who simply accept others as they are

Believe you know yourself better than others

Not freely disclose your views, likes, and dislikes

Prefer not to dwell on the past or worry about the future

Be very self-confident

Think others are entitled to their opinions of you,
but it doesn't matter that much to you

And you may say things like...

"I'm lucky; things
just seem to usually
work out for me..."

"It doesn't do any good
to engage in a lot of
hand-wringing about
what went wrong..."

"I know what's
best for me..."

Now you know a little more about Self-Awareness. Is it about knowing yourself? Absolutely. But it's also about knowing where you want to be. And that through feedback, inward reflection, and applying course corrections where needed, you'll have a really good chance of getting there.

We know that Self-Awareness is a set of skills and attitudes that can be developed. The next section in this chapter focuses on how you can sharpen your Self-Awareness. So if you're wondering what it takes to increase Self-Awareness, demonstrate it more, or make sure you don't overuse it, read on.

Sharpening
your
Self-Awareness

What Can Sometimes Get in the Way of Demonstrating Self-Awareness

Before exploring ways to sharpen your Self-Awareness, it's helpful to think about what may cause you to demonstrate less of this particular agility on a regular basis. Check the causes here that might apply to you. Think about what it looks like and how it may play out in certain situations. And remember that all of these can be addressed if you are motivated to do so.

What might apply to you...

Prefer to keep the focus off yourself

Don't take time for personal reflection

A private person

Unsure how to go about getting feedback

Have trouble reading others' reactions

Not concerned with what others think

Uncomfortable with possible discovery of weaknesses

Not very ambitious

Ways to Sharpen Your Self-Awareness...
Be a Feedback Seeker

Get a broad perspective from others

Solicit formal and informal feedback from different groups you interact with. At work, for instance, different groups can offer unique insights into your strengths and weaknesses. Bosses usually spot things like how well you grasp strategy, your ability to manage up, and your clarity of thinking. Customers can generally gauge your responsiveness, listening, and how well you understand their business needs. Peers see how much you seek common ground, keep the interests of the organization in mind, and follow through on promises. People who report to you are best at noticing the day-to-day behaviors of leadership, like team building, delegating, confronting, approachability, and time use.

Accept feedback as a gift

Nothing discourages feedback more than defensiveness, resistance, irritation, and excuses. People don't like giving feedback anyway, and much less to those who don't listen or are unreceptive. So regardless of the feedback, listen to it and accept it for what it is. Don't say the feedback is inaccurate or a one-time failing; don't argue or qualify. Simply take it in. Use mental rehearsals to get ready for what may happen. If you comment at all, give an example of the behavior being described to validate what they are saying. Chances are good they are right.

Approach every interaction as a way to self-check

How was my approach? What could I have done differently? Especially in areas that you are working on or that are critical to your performance, ask others who have watched you to share feedback with you shortly after events happen. Make this a habit. Seeking feedback increases both the accuracy of your self-understanding and people's evaluation of your overall effectiveness.

Ways to Sharpen Your Self-Awareness...
Turn the Lens Inward

**Complete a
self-inventory**

The goal of Self-Awareness is full knowledge. The good, the bad, and the ugly. What are your clear strengths and how can you use them more effectively? What do you overdo? What strengths have you been previously unaware of? What are known weaknesses? What are untested areas? What are you just OK at? And, most importantly, what are your blind spots—those areas where you see yourself as much more skilled than others see you. It is blind spots, above all else, that stall and derail careers. A goal should be to decrease or eliminate as many things that others see but you don't see.

Be introspective

Why am I perceived this way? How did my strengths get to be so dominant? Are my weaknesses things I avoid, things I'm simply not skilled at, things I dislike, or things I've never done? What experiences have shaped my behavioral patterns? Do I have weaknesses that are related to my strengths, such as the smart person who makes others feel inferior? Use this analysis to determine what is relatively easier and tougher for you to do.

Think about why you judge others the way you do

Knowing what's behind your reactions to others helps you articulate your own behaviors and attitudes. List the people you like and those you dislike and try to find out why. What do those you like have in common with each other and with you? What do those you dislike have in common with each other and how do they differ from you? Are your "people buckets" logical and productive or do they interfere? Could you be more effective without putting people into buckets? Understanding why you react as you do will help you articulate your own behaviors and attitudes.

Ways to Sharpen Your Self-Awareness...
Start the Journey

Keep a learning journal

Log the issues and opportunities you've faced and how you've acted or reacted. Focus on how you've used your strengths or how your weaknesses may have showed up, and why. Use the journal to also record events that triggered strong emotions and reflect on why you responded the way you did. Think through how you came across during interactions with others. Figure out what worked and what didn't and how you would have done it differently. Turn these into rules of thumb to put on display the next time around.

Disclose more   If you deny, minimize, or excuse away mistakes and shortcomings, take a chance and admit that you're imperfect like everyone else. The courage it takes to show you're vulnerable may actually improve others' perceptions of you. Let your inside thoughts out in the open more often. Sprinkle normal work conversation with doubts, what you're thinking about, and what's getting in the way. Select three people who are good at admitting mistakes and shortcomings and observe how they do it.

Find natural mentors   Natural mentors have a special relationship with you and are interested in your success and your future. At work, don't limit yourself to formal mentoring programs, which can be very helpful but may not be immediately available. Try to find people who are not in your direct chain of command, such as a leader you admire or a trusted peer. This will help you have more open, relaxed, and fruitful discussions about yourself and your aspirations. Natural mentors can be a very important source for candid or critical feedback others may not give you.

Be Mindful Not to Overuse Self-Awareness

Too much of most anything isn't necessarily a good thing. The same holds true for Self-Awareness.

While there is much about being self-aware that is helpful, flexing this agility indiscriminately may hurt group process or cause issues with relationships. Left unchecked, overusing Self-Awareness could minimize or erase its benefits altogether.

People who overuse their Self-Awareness may...

Be self-critical to the point of risking credibility and appearing insecure

Become known as a self-help junkie

Divulge personal information that makes others uncomfortable

Solicit feedback indiscriminately and seemingly without purpose

Become dependent on feedback to the point that no moves are made without it

As you focus on building Self-Awareness, temper potential overuse in these ways...

Establish a benchmark for amount of
feedback to take in; once you pass that
threshold in a given situation, move on

Disclose personal information that
is only relevant and helpful to
the given situation

Prioritize then focus on the few areas you
want to work on—the ones that will help
you reach your goals

Create a feedback cadre to serve as your
go-to resources for input

Keep a balanced view of your strengths
and weaknesses

For more help balancing possible Self-Awareness overuse, read
"Execute, Execute, Execute" in the Results Agility chapter, and
"Know People" in the People Agility chapter.

Assignments to Build and Reinforce Self-Awareness

On the Job

Challenge your perception of your skills through an international assignment. In this new and unfamiliar context, cultural missteps are almost a given. Treat those mistakes as opportunities—get feedback on what went wrong, reflect, and learn what to do differently the next time.

Take on a cross-move—an assignment that presents a very different set of challenges, an abrupt shift in tasks/activities, or a new setting and conditions. All these should provide opportunities to get and act on feedback from others.

Start up something new that requires you to forge a new team and build new skills as you go. Because you'll be responsible for the outcome, you will have a vested interest in uncovering personal strengths and weaknesses that will help or hinder success.

On or Off the Job

Make peace with an enemy or someone you've disappointed or someone you've had some trouble with or don't get along with very well. Focus on what you contributed to the situation—not what they did.

Volunteer for a tough and risky project where others have tried but failed. You will soon discover where your own skill gaps may be.

Attend a self-awareness workshop that includes 360° and live, in-class feedback to begin seeing yourself as others see you.

Read More About Self-Awareness

Angelou, M. (2004). *The Collected Autobiographies of Maya Angelou.* **New York, NY: Modern Library.**
This anthology includes the six autobiographical memoirs of Maya Angelou. Rich in imagery, humor, and evocative language, the self-told story of Angelou's journey has inspired people to embrace life with commitment and passion.

Blakeley, K. (2007). *Leadership Blind Spots and What to Do About Them.* **West Sussex, England: John Wiley & Sons.**
This book explores the problems of having blind spots which impede us from adapting, learning, growing, and changing. It offers practices to overcome blind spots in order to perform better in today's competitive global environment.

Cashman, K. (2008). *Leadership from the Inside Out: Becoming a Leader for Life* **(2nd ed.). San Francisco, CA: Berrett-Koehler.**
Leadership from the Inside Out demonstrates the importance of a whole-person approach—leaders can learn to be aware of their core talents, values, and purposes to enhance their energy and effectiveness.

George, B., & Sims, P. (2007). *True North: Discover Your Authentic Leadership.* **San Francisco, CA: Jossey-Bass.**
True North offers an opportunity to become an authentic leader through (1) knowing your authentic self, (2) defining your values and leadership principles, (3) understanding your motivations, (4) building your support team, and (5) staying grounded by integrating all aspects of your life.

Pearman, R. P., Lombardo, M. M., & Eichinger, R. W. (2005). *You: Being More Effective in Your MBTI® Type.* **Minneapolis, MN: Lominger International: A Korn/Ferry Company.**

This research-based leadership development book is built around the 16 personality types assessed by the Myers-Briggs Type Indicator® instrument. It helps individuals to know themselves and others better by discovering their typical strengths, patterns of behavior, and challenges for each type.

Peck, D. (2008). *Beyond Effective: Practices in Self-Aware Leadership.* **Victoria, BC, Canada: Trafford.**

Self-aware leaders usually share the following qualities: deliberate and high-performing core beliefs, humility / open-mindedness, balance between realism and vision, authenticity of heart and mind, and unwavering commitment. The hundred practices in this book help you to confront blind spots, become aware of them, and learn to be more adaptive and skillful.

"I've learned that I still have a lot to learn."

– Maya Angelou

Learning Agility Factor

The extent to which an individual embraces complexity, examines problems in unique and unusual ways, is inquisitive, and can make fresh connections between different concepts

Mental Agility

"To raise new questions, new possibilities, to regard old problems from a new angle, requires creative imagination and marks real advance in science."

Albert Einstein – German-born American physicist and Nobel Prize winner

Was It All IQ?

Albert Einstein. His accomplishments and contributions to science and the world are well known and documented. Though he never took an IQ test, his status as a genius is a given. But how did his thinking take shape? Was it that he was just that much smarter than the rest of us? What was it that enabled Dr. Einstein to open up vistas in his mind that would stump others?

We know the results of Einstein's thinking. What is perhaps less known is *how* he went about thinking through problems. And it's this *how* that is integral to Mental Agility—approaching ambiguous problems in new, creative ways, driven by inquisitiveness and a tireless probing for answers.

So right about now you might be thinking, "Well, since I'm no Einstein, I guess I'm not mentally agile." Not true! It turns out that for most of us, IQ and Mental Agility aren't that closely related. Einstein certainly possessed a superior intellect, but his problem-solving strategies are ones that we can all use.

A strong believer in the value of curiosity, Einstein approached life in general and science in particular with an inquisitive eye. As a small child, he became mesmerized by the physical properties of a simple compass. He wondered how the compass could be controlled by something not visible to the naked eye and came to the conclusion that "something deeply hidden had to be behind things." This passionate curiosity showed up as persistent and progressively deeper levels of questioning throughout Einstein's life.

As described by a close family friend, Einstein was able to "see many, many dimensions *and* could see the whole." Well-read in a broad array of topics, including philosophy, Einstein was a true big-picture thinker. He framed problems by visualizing them—using pictures, diagrams, and icons in lieu of numbers and words. Perhaps because he approached problem solving by visualization, he was able to distill his ideas so they could be more easily understood. Einstein has sometimes been quoted as describing it this way: "If you can't explain it simply, you don't understand it well enough." He became very adept at applying pictures or metaphors to even the most complex scientific topics, which helped make his ideas more accessible to others.

Albert Einstein is a classic example of Mental Agility in action. But while Einstein himself was certainly unique, the qualities that made him mentally agile are ones that can be readily found in others as well. Einstein embodies Mental Agility, not due to a purportedly ultrahigh IQ, but because of *how* he thought through issues and searched for answers.

Why Mental Agility Matters

Today's world is arguably even more complex than the one in which Einstein lived. Complexity that comes in the form of increasingly rapid technological advancements, global connectedness, and shifts in market dominance, to name a few. Increasing complexity means the problems you face are often more intricate, your opportunities more elusive.

Nowhere is this more evident than the world of work. You may face complex problems like these on a daily basis: How do we jump-start sales? What new markets will we enter and why? How will we address that thorny labor-relations issue that refuses to go away? Success in business depends on figuring out the best solution to difficult, high-stakes issues. Issues that are often ambiguous—offering either insufficient information or maybe too much information. Potential solutions may require very different approaches yet have comparable costs, efforts, and risks. There's rarely one clearly correct answer.

With the growing and changing demands in business today and in the future, a person who possesses Mental Agility will be increasingly valued as a creative and resourceful problem solver in the organization. A healthy skepticism of favorite past solutions keeps the mentally agile mind open to new possibilities and fresh connections. With curiosity to fuel new ideas and gain a deeper understanding of issues, it becomes easier to define problems in more than superficial ways.

The mentally agile person has the unique ability to hold in his or her mind multiple and varied characteristics of a situation while simultaneously grasping the essence of it. This duality in thinking becomes a powerful combination for defining problems that can then be crisply articulated. This is part of the elegance of applied Mental Agility—making the complex accessible to others. People who offer truly simple explanations and solutions to a complex problem must have a clear understanding of its complexity first.

If you are on the higher end of the Mental Agility continuum

You are likely to...

Be curious and inquisitive

Enjoy exploring the new

Delve deeply into problems

Look for parallels and contrasts

Search for the meaning below the surface

Sift through complexity and quickly grasp the essence of issues

Express the complex in simple, easy-to-understand ways

Help others think things through

And you may say things like...

"This issue reminds me of
something I read recently
in the biography of..."

"I was curious to see if there
were similarities or contrasts
between this problem and..."

"Another way to
look at this is..."

If you demonstrate
Mental Agility less often

You may...

Favor well-established solutions

Prefer to move to solutions quickly

Focus on what is readily apparent when examining issues

View problems from your own unique point of view

Value conventional wisdom when addressing situations

Prefer when things aren't messy and uncertain

Know instinctively what the best answer is without needing to explain it

Seek solutions that are mostly error-proof

And you may say things like...

"Let's stick with the
proven approach..."

"It's plain to see what
the solution is..."

"This is risky—I
want to be certain
that we get it right..."

Now you know a little more about Mental Agility. It's not about traditional book smarts. It's about being curious, getting comfortable with complexity and ambiguity, and digging into problems with a fresh perspective.

We know that Mental Agility is a set of skills and attitudes that can be developed. The next section in this chapter focuses on how you can sharpen your Mental Agility. So if you're wondering what it takes to increase Mental Agility, demonstrate it more, or make sure you don't overuse it, read on.

Sharpening
your
Mental Agility

What Can Sometimes Get in the Way of Demonstrating Mental Agility

Before exploring ways to sharpen your Mental Agility, it's helpful to think about what may cause you to demonstrate less of this particular agility on a regular basis. Check the causes here that might apply to you. Think about what it looks like and how it may play out in certain situations. And remember that all of these can be addressed if you are motivated to do so.

What might apply to you...

More comfortable solving problems than digging into them

Less comfortable with uncertainty

Have a limited range of experiences

Highly specialized in one area

Stuck in the past

Have and express strong opinions

Stick with set patterns of thinking

Lack disciplined problem solving

Appear closed to others' perspectives

Default to favorite solutions

Ways to Sharpen Your Mental Agility...
Fight Sameness

Expose yourself to the unfamiliar

Attend perspective-broadening lectures and workshops on topics that you normally don't attend. Go to the theater, concerts, and other cultures' festivals. Travel to and vacation in different locales. Change up day-to-day things—drive to work a different way, use the computer mouse with your opposite hand, rearrange your furniture. Stimulate your brain by doing things, going places, and talking to people outside of your routine. Constantly ask yourself, is there anything new to learn here? Anything that may surprise me?

Purposefully look beyond the obvious

Look under rocks for the new, different, and unique. If you're typically logical, be outrageous and silly. Flip on your imagination switch that may have gone dormant over time. Think like a child. Ask why again and again. Extend yourself. Be courageous and propose things that may seem revolutionary to some.

Get out of your comfort zone

Many busy people rely too much on solutions from their own history. They rely on what has happened to them in the past. Using this limited lens, they are quick to see sameness in problems that isn't necessarily there. Beware of "I have always..." or "Usually I..." Always pause, consider alternatives, and ask yourself, is this really like the problems I have solved in the past? Or, conversely, how is this different from past problems?

Ways to Sharpen Your Mental Agility...
Embrace the Unknown

Visualize the problem

Complex processes or problems with a lot of uncertainty are hard to understand. They tend to be a hopeless maze unless they are put in a visual format. One technique is a pictorial chart, called a storyboard, where a process or vision or strategy is illustrated by its components being depicted as pictures. Not a visual person? A variation of this is to do the old pro and con, +'s and –'s of a problem or process, then flow chart those according to what's working and not working.

Ask more questions

Studies have shown that about 50% of discussions involve answers; only 7% involve probing questions. Questions that get people thinking, that tease out important data. Questions like: Why does that work? Why might my solution not work this time? How would I know if it did or didn't? What's least likely? What's missing from the problem?

Don't try to get it totally right the first time

If a situation is ambiguous, be incremental. Make a small decision; get instant feedback. Correct the course, get a little more data, move forward a little more until the bigger problem is under control. Treat mistakes and failures as ways to learn. Focus on your third or fourth try, not the first.

Ways to Sharpen Your Mental Agility...
Think It Through

Check for common errors in thinking

Do you state as facts things that are really opinions or assumptions? Before you speak, make sure your assertions are fact-based. Do you attribute cause and effect to relationships when you don't know if one causes the other? If sales are down, and we increase advertising and sales go up, this doesn't prove causality. They are simply related. Overgeneralizing is another common error. If you generalize from a single example, you risk shutting down new ideas.

Dig for root causes

Keep asking why. See how many causes you can come up with and how many organizing buckets you can put them in. This increases the chance of a better solution because you can see more connections. Chess masters recognize thousands of possible patterns of chess pieces. Look for patterns in data; don't just collect information.

Look for parallels in personal, organization, or the world, in general successes and failures

What was common to each success? What was present in each failure but never present in a success? Focus more on the successes; failures are easier to analyze but don't in themselves tell you what would work. Comparing successes, while less exciting, yields more information about underlying principles. The bottom line is to reduce your insights to principles or rules of thumb you think might be repeatable. When faced with the next new problem, those general underlying principles will apply again.

Be Mindful Not to Overuse Mental Agility

Too much of most anything isn't necessarily a good thing. The same holds true for Mental Agility.

While there is much about being mentally agile that is helpful, flexing this agility indiscriminately may hurt group process or cause issues with relationships. Left unchecked, overusing Mental Agility could minimize or erase its benefits altogether.

People who overuse their Mental Agility may...

Get infatuated with marginally productive ideas simply because they are new

See connections or insist on filling in gaps by adding things that aren't there

Assume that even the simplest of problems must have deeper, hidden complexity

Get so caught up in problem exploration that deadlines are missed

View their own ideas as superior to others

As you focus on building Mental Agility, temper potential overuse in these ways...

Moderate your idea-processing speed so others have a chance to catch up

Avoid overcomplicating things; focus instead on making the complex simple

Be patient; give due process its due

Don't dismiss proven solutions indiscriminately in favor of the new and different—chances are they are proven with good reason

Recognize that efficient solutions can also be effective ones

For more help balancing possible Mental Agility overuse, read "Adapt to People" in the People Agility chapter, and "Be a Feedback Seeker" in the Self-Awareness chapter.

Assignments to Build
and Reinforce Mental Agility

On the Job

Tackle a fix-it assignment that calls for lots of decisions to be made on incomplete data in a short time frame. This will help you practice experimenting with small, creative solutions, evaluate how well they work, regroup, and try again.

Find an opportunity to work in a strategic planning role which will provide you with a treasure trove of opportunities to make fresh connections, analyze multiple new ideas, and devise new ways of looking at old problems.

Increase the scope of your typical assignment. This will provide you with broader exposure to variety, complexity, and uncertainty. Rather than applying your past decisions indiscriminately, evaluate them in the context of this new, bigger world to see if they are still the best option.

On or Off the Job

Work on a team that has to integrate diverse systems,
processes, or procedures where you will need to
understand both the component pieces and
the whole picture of how the pieces can
work together.

Lobby for a cause on a contested issue
in local, regional, state, or federal government.
This will expose you to different perspectives
and complex issues with no easy answers.

Lead a team involved with a project where you
know the least about the subject to practice
curiosity and stretch your perspective beyond
your comfort zone.

Read More About Mental Agility

Hurson, T. (2007). *Think Better: An Innovator's Guide to Productive Thinking.* **New York, NY: McGraw-Hill.**
Productive thinking is an attitude that examines problems and converts them into opportunities. The author offers a model to help readers think creatively and critically, stay with the question, strive for more ideas, look for connections, and forge the best solution.

International Herald Tribune. **http://www.iht.com**
The *International Herald Tribune* is a widely read English international newspaper. It offers international headlines which help readers gain broader perspectives.

Martin, R. (2007). *The Opposable Mind: How Successful Leaders Win Through Integrative Thinking.* **Boston, MA: Harvard Business School Press.**
Integrative thinking is the ability to hold two opposing ideas at once and synthesize the ideas to improve each position. This book provides readers with strategies to develop integrative thinking using integrative tools combined with their own experience.

Michalko, M. (2011). *Creative Thinkering: Putting Your Imagination to Work.* **Novato, CA: New World Library.**
The key to creatively generating associations and connections between dissimilar subjects is conceptual thinking. Through exercises, strategies, and real-world examples, the author shows how to develop the imagination, synthesize dissimilar subjects, think paradoxically, and enlist the help of the subconscious mind.

Pink, D. (2006). *A Whole New Mind: Why Right-Brainers Will Rule the Future.* **New York, NY: Penguin Group.**
Right-brain thinkers are creative, recognize patterns, and make meaning from the patterns. Pink explores six crucial aptitudes to help expand our ways of thinking to create a whole new mind—one that will rule the future.

Wilkinson, D. (2006). *The Ambiguity Advantage: What Great Leaders Are Great At.* **Hampshire, England: Palgrave Macmillan.**
Understanding and dealing with ambiguity is what differentiates successful leaders from the rest. This book describes how to move into a future of change with more confidence, how to gain advantage from ambiguity, and how to lead others through uncertainty and ambiguity.

"The important thing is not to stop questioning; curiosity has its own reason for existing."

– Albert Einstein

The degree to which one is open-minded toward others, enjoys interacting with a diversity of people, understands their unique strengths, interests, and limitations, and uses them effectively to accomplish organizational goals

People
Agility

"If you talk to a man in a language he understands, that goes to his head. If you talk to him in his language, that goes to his heart."

Nelson Mandela – Former South African president

What Could Move
an Immovable Object?

Nelson Mandela. A man who symbolizes triumph over adversity. A man central in the decades-long struggle and eventual victory over systemic racial segregation and oppression in South Africa. Imprisoned for more than 27 years, Mandela emerged a larger-than-life persona, having won the respect of unlikely sources—from his jailors to government leaders. How was he able to accomplish this feat? How did he win over those who opposed him? And influence their actions to such an extent that he was freed and his cause soon won?

During his imprisonment, Mandela became known for striking a tone of mutual understanding with the opposition in general and his jailors in particular. Some of his followers saw this as a sign of weakness. But Mandela knew that the best way to move a person's opinion was by first understanding how that opinion was formed. He did this in many ways—learning Afrikaans, the ruling party's native language, reading their poetry, studying their history, even following their sports teams. Through this study, Mandela discovered that, fundamentally, there was much in common between the opposing groups. Having this broader, more inclusive perspective allowed Mandela to make inroads with the opposition—small at first and, ultimately, historic.

Mandela is a student of people. In people interactions, he has shown that he values people while maintaining a personal authenticity. In prison, the most potent example of this was his commitment to learning Afrikaans so he could converse in the language of his jailors. Why? To remove barriers and to help build relationships. By modeling respect without being submissive, Mandela expected respect in return. And, in time, he got it. In later negotiations with the ruling party, Mandela adopted a blunt yet courteous communication style. Blunt because he knew that Afrikaners are generally blunt and respect bluntness in others. Courteous because that is a personal value of Mandela's.

Studying rugby scores to converse with a prison commander. Interpreting Afrikaner poetry to see things from another's perspective. Donning a team's rugby jersey that had previously been a symbol of apartheid to encourage reconciliation. These examples and more show how Mandela was able to, in his words, "address their hearts." By making it a priority to know people, adapt to them, meet them more than halfway and, at its root, value them, Mandela was able to accomplish great things. These qualities are the common thread in those with People Agility.

Why People Agility Matters

"I'm a people person!" Chances are you've either uttered this statement yourself or heard it countless times from others. There's nothing wrong with this phrase other than it's a bit hard to pin down exactly what being a "people person" looks like or exactly how it adds value. People Agility, on the other hand, offers many tangible benefits and is fairly easy to spot in action.

Being people agile means being a student. A student of people. How? By seeking to not just understand another's perspective, but to understand what life experiences, motivations, and values shaped that perspective. With this knowledge, you can then decode, distill, and compare others' viewpoints to your own.

A key to getting anything of value done is the ability to see differences in people and to use those differences for everyone's benefit. This is especially helpful in conflict situations. At minimum, you gain an appreciation of others' views. And in many cases you end up finding much in common, which helps get the conflict resolved to everyone's satisfaction.

Part of being people agile is meeting each person where he or she is to get done what you need to get done. Doing this in the moment means really listening—suspending your own agenda so you can read and respond to the signals of others. It means staying tuned in—and not just to those with perceived special status. By adjusting your approach to meet the needs of others, you make a strong statement that you value them—and they will respect and trust you in return.

People Agility means factoring people into your priorities—for their good, for your good and, at work, for the organization's good. Demonstrate that you value others and you'll end up reaping the rewards. Rewards like more allies. Faster buy-in for your ideas. Less noise around change. People Agility makes it easier for you to get things done when getting things done involves others. And frankly, it almost always involves others.

If you are on the higher end of the People Agility continuum

You are likely to...

Relate well to all kinds of people

Read situations quickly

Pay attention to what people have to say

Defuse high-tension situations comfortably

Embrace and leverage diversity of people and viewpoints

Navigate political waters effectively

Get things done effectively with and through
different types of people

Adjust your approach depending upon others'
needs and preferences

Explain the viewpoints of others accurately

Confront interpersonal conflict productively

And you may say things like...

"Really enjoyed our chat
yesterday! Speaking of that,
what do you think of this idea
to help out your situation...?"

"Let me see
if I understand
your position..."

"What are your ideas
on this...?"

If you demonstrate People Agility less often

You may...

Approach people situations in a consistent, steadfast way

Do and say things that align with your personal values and code of conduct

Think business and personal lives are meant to be entirely separate

Favor harmony

Like to work and socialize with people you have a lot in common with

Prefer to let conflicts work themselves out

Value when roles, rules of interaction, and responsibilities are well defined

Treat everyone the same

Avoid situations that appear political in nature

Prefer working alone and being accountable for your own contributions

And you may say things like...

"We wasted so much time talking
about her weekend that I was
late for my next meeting..."

"Let's just agree
to disagree..."

"His position just doesn't
make sense based on what
I know to be right..."

Now you know a little more about People Agility. It's not necessarily about being extraverted, outgoing, gregarious, or fun at parties. It's about knowing and valuing people. And using that knowledge not for purely selfish purposes, but in ways that help build relationships and, by extension, get things done.

We know that People Agility is a set of skills and attitudes that can be developed. The next section in this chapter focuses on how you can sharpen your People Agility. So if you're wondering what it takes to increase People Agility, demonstrate it more, or make sure you don't overuse it, read on.

Sharpening
your
People Agility

What Can Sometimes Get in the Way of Demonstrating People Agility

Before exploring ways to sharpen your People Agility, it's helpful to think about what may cause you to demonstrate less of this particular agility on a regular basis. Check the causes here that might apply to you. Think about what it looks like and how it may play out in certain situations. And remember that all of these can be addressed if you are motivated to do so.

What might apply to you...

Impatient

Being true to yourself is an overriding concern

Think consistency is a virtue

Think others should adjust to you

Better at working with data and things

Difficulty reading others' verbal and nonverbal cues

Uncomfortable with face-to-face conflict

Take things personally

Don't make others a priority

Get stressed or overwhelmed easily

Ways to Sharpen Your People Agility...
Value People

Manage the first three minutes

This is essential in any interaction. The tone is set. First impressions are formed. Work on being more open and approachable, and take in more information during the beginning of a transaction. Put others at ease so that they feel OK about disclosing. Initiate rapport, listening, sharing, understanding, even comforting. Approachable people get more information, know things earlier, and can get others to do more things. The more you can get others to initiate and say early in the interaction, the more you'll know about their intentions and the better you can tailor your approach.

Be fully present
More than 50% of our communication power is visual, so your nonverbal cues probably speak volumes. If you're not fully engaged in interactions, it may show up as a blank stare, interrupting, your impatient "I'm busy" look, or constantly checking your phone. Most around you know your signs. Do you? Ask someone you trust what it is you do when they think you are not listening. Not a face-to-face interaction? People can still tell when you're not fully present. On phone calls, it's the multitasking that gets you: from the obvious—typing heard in the background, to the more subtle—asking questions already answered or not tracking with the flow of the conversation.

Share more
Confide your thinking on an issue and invite the response of others. Pass on information nuggets that will help people do their jobs better or broaden their perspectives. Share more than just what people need to know to do their jobs. What sharing would be genuinely interesting to them? Help them feel valued? Work to know and remember important things about the people you work around, for, and with. Establish things you can talk about with each person outside of the topic at hand. This is pure equity in action—share more information and you will get more in return.

Ways to Sharpen Your People Agility...
Know People

Approach situations from the outside in

Start from the perspective of others (the customer, the audience, the person, the situation), not from the inside out ("What do *I* want to do in this situation; what would make *me* happy and feel good?"). Think about what's at stake for the people involved in a given situation. How does this person or audience best learn? Which of my approaches or styles would work best? How can I alter my approach and tactics to be the most effective? People respond favorably to ease of transaction, so meet them where they are.

Seek out others who are not like you

It's tempting to gravitate to those you feel most comfortable with. It's likely they are similar in personality, political views, and skill set. But there's not much you can learn from an echo of yourself. Instead, seek out variety, people whom you wouldn't ordinarily associate with or have little in common with. Even someone who grates on you or whom you often disagree with. What do others like or see in that person? Work on understanding what they do well and not well, what's behind their actions and viewpoints.

Think through or even present the viewpoints of others

How did they form those viewpoints? Are there underlying values at play? If you were in their shoes, would you have come to the same conclusion? What do they not know that prevented them from coming to your conclusion? Or, what don't *you* know that has stopped you from adopting their views? By gaining understanding of others' perspectives, you expand your own.

Ways to Sharpen Your People Agility...
Adapt to People

Tailor your approach to fit others' needs

Don't just tell and sell. Be able to clearly state others' views. Vary your approach depending on whom you're interacting with. If you're a marketing person speaking with engineers, learn their conceptual categories by asking them how they would analyze it and what questions they would ask. Regardless of audience, some common questions to consider are: What's their time tolerance? Do they prefer formal or informal interactions? Would they rather just chat about the topic? How sophisticated is the group? How much pushback do you expect?

Home in on people's responses

Check in with your audience frequently and select a different tactic if necessary. Monitor the reactions of people to what you are doing and saying. If they're bored, change the pace. Confused? State your argument differently. Angry? Stop and find out what's going on. Too quiet? Ask questions to get them engaged. Disinterested? Figure out what's in it for them. Be vigilant and be ready to adjust your interpersonal style and approach so that everyone gets something useful out of the time.

Turn conflicts into collaborations

The surest way to make conflict constructive is to demonstrate equity—making others feel understood and respected and taking a problem-oriented approach. This means being able to state others' positions as clearly as they do, giving them legitimacy. Generate lots of possibilities. Find common ground within those before staking out a position. Ask lots of questions, speak briefly, summarize often. Frame disagreements in conditional terms ("I don't think so, but what do you think?"). This gives the other person a chance to apply his or her perspective. Handling disagreements this way achieves two goals—resolution of the problem at hand and data to load into your approaches file for future interactions.

Be Mindful Not to Overuse People Agility

Too much of most anything isn't necessarily a good thing. The same holds true for People Agility.

While there is much about being people agile that is helpful, flexing this agility indiscriminately may hurt group process or cause issues with relationships. Left unchecked, overusing People Agility could minimize or erase its benefits altogether.

People who overuse their People Agility may...

Spend too much time building networks at the expense of getting things done

Be perceived as too political and ambitious

Show different faces to different people, causing some people to be confused and others to not trust them

Rely too heavily on relationships and hesitate being firm for fear of damaging those relationships

Shift situationally so easily that they leave the impression of being wishy-washy

As you focus on building People Agility, temper potential overuse in these ways...

Be an equal opportunity adaptor so those
you interact with don't feel you only value
the movers and shakers

Balance people inclusiveness with speed
when moving things forward

Take a stand on tough issues
when warranted

Be authentic in interactions so
others have a consistent baseline
perception of you

Articulate a position once others
feel they have been heard

For more help balancing possible People Agility overuse, read "Be a Feedback Seeker" in the Self-Awareness chapter.

Assignments to Build
and Reinforce People Agility

On the Job

Seek out a cross-move assignment that requires working with a new group of people from another function with a different background and viewpoint. Gain an understanding of those differing perspectives to build solid relationships in order to get things done.

Influence without authority by taking on a staff assignment that involves working across organizational boundaries where people and political skills are at a premium.

Go global with an international assignment that provides exposure to conflicting cultures and a new and diverse population. Take time to not just understand the other culture, but to compare and contrast it with your own. This will help you relate effectively to those you interact closely with.

On or Off the Job

Volunteer to work for a charity or community organization to build your experiences with a broader spectrum of people—for example, younger or older than you, different cultures, different neighborhoods, or different economic status.

Lead a project team or task force where the other people in the group are towering experts but you aren't. You will need to gain an understanding of their viewpoints on the subject and leverage those to be successful.

Manage a dissatisfied internal or external customer where moving from conflict to satisfaction or collaboration is crucial. Play out the situation from the customer's viewpoint—you're likely to unearth common ground and a better understanding of what is behind their dissatisfaction.

Read More About People Agility

Bradberry, T., & Greaves, J. (2009). *Emotional Intelligence 2.0.* **San Diego, CA: TalentSmart**[®].
Emotional intelligence includes four core EQ skills (self-awareness, self-management, social awareness, and relationship management) that are crucial for personal and professional success. This book provides practical findings and insights on how to develop EQ.

Brent, M., & Dent, F. (2010). *The Leader's Guide to Influence: How to Use Soft Skills to Get Hard Results.* **Harlow, UK: Pearson.**
This book is intended to help leaders and managers better understand the communication and influence aspects of managing various work relationships. It provides real-life lessons learned from many leaders in developing and maintaining effective working relationships.

Dimitrius, J., & Mazzarella, W. P. (2008). *Reading People: How to Understand People and Predict Their Behavior—Anytime, Anyplace* **(Rev. ed.). New York, NY: Ballantine.**
The key to reading people effectively is to objectively observe and identify behavioral clues and see patterns within those clues. This book describes how to gather behavioral clues from appearance, body language, voice, communication style, and content.

Gerzon, M. (2006). *Leading Through Conflict: How Successful Leaders Transform Differences into Opportunities.* **Boston, MA: Harvard Business School Press.**
This book features how we can choose to respond to conflict, which is an act of leadership. The author suggests

how readers can face differences honestly and creatively, understand the complexity and scope of differences, and turn conflicts into opportunities for collaboration and innovation.

Klaus, P. (2007). *The Hard Truth About Soft Skills: Workplace Lessons Smart People Wish They'd Learned Sooner.* **New York, NY: HarperCollins Publishers.**
Soft skills are often neglected, but they are crucial because they will impact individuals' careers and promotions. This book provides insights, strategies, and techniques to develop and enhance soft skill areas: communicating, getting jobs done, handling critics, politics, leadership, dealing with differences, and self-promotion.

Mandela, N. (1995). *Long Walk to Freedom: The Autobiography of Nelson Mandela.* **New York, NY: Little, Brown & Company.**
This book profiles Mandela's early life, coming of age, education, and 27 years in prison. The last chapters include stories of his path to liberation and eventual leadership of South Africa.

"Know your enemy— and learn about his favorite sport."

– Nelson Mandela

Learning Agility Factor

The extent to which
an individual likes change,
continuously explores new
options and solutions, and
is interested in leading
organizational change efforts

Change
Agility

"If we are not achieving something, it is because we have not put our minds to it. We create what we want."

Muhammad Yunus – Bengali founder of Grameen Bank

Where Can "What Ifs" Lead?

Muhammad Yunus. Founder of the Grameen Bank and father of the microlending model now used globally. Self-described banker to the poor. Through his philosophy and practice of microlending, Professor Yunus turned conventional banking on its head—with life-changing results for the bank's millions of borrowers, most of whom are women. But where did Yunus' revolutionary ideas come from? And how was he able to transform those ideas into a growing and thriving enterprise that offers real solutions to help lift so many out of poverty?

A professor of rural economics in his native Bangladesh, Yunus understood the problem of systemic poverty in his country. Incensed by a particularly cruel money-lending practice he witnessed, he lent the equivalent of US$27 to a group of village stool makers so they could buy materials and sell their products at a fair price—which they did. This small act became the impetus for an experiment with his students to try and repeat the process on a larger scale. And from that small experiment more followed, finally growing into the Grameen Bank as it is today.

By connecting what he knew—economics and Bengali culture— with what in many ways is the opposite of conventional banking norms, Yunus created a new way to think about banks and banking. He faced resistance to these changes along the way—from husbands and village elders to traditional banks and social development agencies. As the bank grew, he tried out different ideas and processes. Some worked, others didn't. But even today, Yunus keeps the ideas coming.

Then and now, Yunus continually poses the big questions: What if…? Why? Why not? When the idea for the Grameen Bank was being formed, the question was: "What if we lent a small amount of money to these poor people so they could become independent?" And to conventional bankers: "Why can't we lend without collateral?" Now his what ifs take shape on a global scale as he seeks to realize his vision of a world without poverty.

Like Muhammad Yunus, those with Change Agility are rarely satisfied with the status quo. For Yunus, this took shape as having a really big idea that started off small. Yunus challenged conventional wisdom but used that convention as a springboard for his new ideas. And he tried, had some successes, some failures, corrected course, and kept moving forward. And now his big idea is achieving transformational results.

Why Change Agility Matters

Change. Depending on your perspective, this word can be either exhilarating or anxiety-ridden. For most of us, the reality lies somewhere in between. One thing that is pretty clear today is that change is everywhere and coming at us more quickly all the time. Those with Change Agility are better equipped for this reality because they can embrace, own, and lead change.

The change agile person is able to vision the future—not based on fairy tales or random, creative thought, but as a result of careful study. The study of history and of trends that are starting to take shape. Of parallels and the lessons learned by others. By crafting and evaluating different scenarios, the change agile person increases the chances of acting on target when the future gets here. Even better, when you're change agile, you have the chance to create the future you want.

So much of what we read about sweeping change and the people who lead change centers on the outcome, the big finish, and less on the journey toward that outcome. But the truth is that most changes come as a result of a long road of trial and error, mistakes, even accidents. Being change agile means you are tirelessly experimenting, putting yourself out there, risking failure because you know that failure equals learning. Learning what not to do the next time you try. Most of the things we use today in life were not created instantly. Instead, they came along as the very last car in a long train of experimentation.

Carrying the change banner can make you unpopular with some in the short-term and others in the long-term. Change is scary, frustrating, and worrisome for many. After all, we're mostly wired to like the comfort zone and to nest build. We like things to stay the same. Those with Change Agility are able to absorb this discomfort, honor the need of others to vent or resist, and still forge ahead with the change they know to be right.

If you are on the higher end of the Change Agility continuum

You are likely to...

Have a passion for ideas

View problems as opportunities for change and improvement

Enjoy experimenting with test cases

Explore ideas and put them into practice

View risk taking as an opportunity for trial and error and learning

Be highly interested in continuous improvement

Remain calm under pressure and times of uncertainty

Handle others' discomfort with change,
and continue to move forward

And you may say things like...

"Why can't it be done...?"

"OK, so this didn't work.
What did we learn that
we can apply...?"

"What if we tried...?"

If you demonstrate
Change Agility less often

You may...

Like it when things are settled

Tend to be skeptical of unvetted ideas

Honor tradition

Favor keeping things the same that seem to be working

Want everyone to like you

Collect and analyze lots of data to be sure of success

Ensure consensus before initiating change

Enjoy tasks that have stability, orderliness, and routine

And you may say things like…

"There's a lot we need to
consider before moving
forward with this…"

"I can't wait till the
day I come in and things
are actually stable…!"

"If it ain't broke,
don't fix it…"

Now you know a little more about Change Agility. It's more than being comfortable with change. It's questioning the way things are in the spirit of making things better. Experimenting with potentially unpopular ideas that may not be fully vetted as a way to learn. And being willing to take the heat that comes with leading change.

We know that Change Agility is a set of skills and attitudes that can be developed. The next section in this chapter focuses on how you can sharpen your Change Agility. So if you're wondering what it takes to increase Change Agility, demonstrate it more, or make sure you don't overuse it, read on.

Sharpening
your
Change Agility

What Can Sometimes Get in the Way of Demonstrating Change Agility

Before exploring ways to sharpen your Change Agility, it's helpful to think about what may cause you to demonstrate less of this particular agility on a regular basis. Check the causes here that might apply to you. Think about what it looks like and how it may play out in certain situations. And remember that all of these can be addressed if you are motivated to do so.

What might apply to you...

Uncomfortable with people conflict

Get easily stressed or anxious

Ill-at-ease being first or out front of others

Most comfortable with what is known

Focus solely on the short-term

Concerned about being criticized or being wrong

Care a lot about what people think

Need to get it right the first time

Avoid risk whenever possible

Have difficulty handling uncertainty

Ways to Sharpen Your Change Agility...
Be an Idea Magnet

Become a
student of
your business

Whether it's the next big idea or a hundred smaller ones that lead to continuous improvement, having a deep, solid understanding of your business is a must. Talk to the people who know. Meet with strategic partners and key customers. Read about your business and industry in the press. Get to know your competitors and your customers' competitors. Reduce your understanding to rules of thumb and use them to visualize initiatives that could make a huge difference.

Make connections to envision the new

Fresh ideas don't spontaneously spring forth from hydroponic ponds. They are planted and nurtured by your experiences and the experiences of those around you. More often, new ideas are a result of cross-pollinating those experiences–making fresh connections that lead to something new. The modern minivan was not dreamed up out of thin air. It was a result of combining the cargo hauling features of full-sized vans with the ride comfort and other consumer-friendly features of a station wagon.

Hunt for parallels outside your usual frame of reference

If you restrict yourself to the connections you currently make, you'll only come up with breakthrough ideas by sheer chance. Life is full of repetition, full of patterns that repeat in adjacent areas of life. Virtually nothing is truly new. Fresh ideas, truly new and unique ideas are unlikely to be found in benchmarking or examining best practices. They're often found by connecting patterns in adjacent and remote domains. Find a parallel situation to the underlying issue–for example, who has to do things really fast (Domino's, FedEx)? Who has to deal with maximum ambiguity (emergency room staff, police dispatchers)? Check out the History Channel's *Modern Marvels*, which answers the question "How did they do that?"

Ways to Sharpen Your Change Agility...
Turn Vision into Reality

Balance perfection with action

If you suspend action until all the information is in, you risk falling into analysis paralysis. Many of us just collect data, which numerous studies show increases our confidence but doesn't increase decision accuracy. Perfectionism is tough to let go of because most people see it as a positive trait for them. Recognize your perfectionism for what it might be—collecting more information than others do to improve your confidence in making a fault-free decision and thereby avoiding risk and criticism.

Be an incrementalist

The most successful innovators try lots of quick, inexpensive experiments to increase the chances of success. The more uncertain the situation is, the more likely it is you will make mistakes in the beginning. Growth and change often require risk, sacrifice, and making errors the first time you try new tasks. The key is to make small decisions, get instant feedback, adjust, and get better. The faster and the more frequent the cycles, the more opportunities to learn.

Work the maze

Creative ideas will be orphans unless they can be transformed into something tangible. To make that happen, you'll likely have to deal with many units outside your immediate area. Organizations can be complex mazes with many turns, dead ends, quick routes, and choices. In most organizations, the best path to get somewhere is almost never a straight line. Since organizations are made up of people, they become all that more complex. There are gatekeepers, expediters, blockers, resisters, guides, Good Samaritans, and influencers. Leading the way through the maze will be key to making your innovation a reality.

Ways to Sharpen Your Change Agility...
Take the Heat

Prepare in advance

Leading is risky. You have to defend what you're doing, so convince yourself first that you are on the right track. Be prepared to explain again and again, to attract lightning bolts from detractors, from those individuals unsettled by change, and from those naysayers who always will argue it could have been done differently, better, faster, or cheaper. To prepare for those possibilities, think about 10 objections that could come up and mentally rehearse how you will reply. Listen patiently to people's concerns, acknowledge them, and then explain why you think this change will be beneficial.

Give others choices

When a proposed change affects us personally, we often experience a highly visceral reaction. Part of this is due to feeling a loss of control. During the change process, the more you can emphasize what is still in a person's control and, when applicable, how the change will help them, the less resistance you're likely to face. So be flexible. How changes can be implemented should be as open as possible. Studies show that people work harder when they have a sense of choice over how they accomplish the new and different.

Manage the message

When leading and communicating change, your primary job is to convey the what and the why. But that doesn't mean bulldozing the people impacted. When confronted with resistance, look for common interests and underlying concerns. Try on their views for size—the emotion as well as the content. Ask yourself if you understand their feelings. Ask what they would do if they were in your shoes. See if you can restate each other's position and advocate it for a minute to get inside each other's place.

Be Mindful Not to Overuse Change Agility

Too much of most anything isn't necessarily a good thing. The same holds true for Change Agility.

While there is much about being change agile that is helpful, flexing this agility indiscriminately may hurt group process or cause issues with relationships. Left unchecked, overusing Change Agility could minimize or erase its benefits altogether.

People who overuse their Change Agility may...

Seek out change simply for change's sake

Disproportionately favor the new and risky at the expense of proven solutions

Undervalue others' need for orderly problem solving, analysis, and careful implementation

Get involved with too many things at once

Marginalize people's legitimate concerns about change; have a change-at-all-costs mentality

As you focus on building Change Agility, temper potential overuse in these ways...

Hear people out

Don't chase every idea like it's
a bright, shiny object; discriminate

Honor history and precedent
when it's warranted

Avoid change overload in others; gauge
the appetite for change in the affected
population and adjust accordingly

Balance forging ahead with proper
analysis and problem-solving due process

For more help balancing possible Change Agility overuse, read "Adapt to People" in the People Agility chapter.

Assignments to Build and Reinforce Change Agility

On the Job

Become a change manager by leading a major effort to change something or implement something of significance that requires others to buy in and cooperate. This will force you to both shape your vision and motivate others to see the value of the change as you do.

Tackle a fix-it or turnaround assignment where you will make tough decisions that will significantly impact a variety of people and constituencies and bring about the need to try a lot of new things. In these assignments, change is a given, so your ability to paint the future vision and execute on it will be critical.

Start something new, whether a project, function, or even a business, that requires the formation of a new team and attempting things for the first time on a tight timetable. Much will be unknown and you will need to navigate the uncertainty and bring others along with you to create something of value.

On or Off the Job

Relaunch an existing product or service that's not doing well. This will require generating and implementing new ideas while securing support from those involved.

Seek out and use a seed budget to create, pursue, and implement an idea you are passionate about. Vet your own passion with others—see if you can make it contagious.

Prepare and present a strategic proposal of some consequence to top management that involves a change in direction. To be successful, you will need to think through why it should be done, how it can be accomplished, and where the stumbling blocks may arise.

Read More About Change Agility

Aitken, P., & Higgs, M. (2010). *Developing Change Leaders: The Principles and Practices of Change Leadership Development.* **Oxford, UK: Butterworth-Heinemann.**

The authors provide a combination of academic research and rich description of how to develop individuals and create a change leader environment. This book will help you assess your readiness for leading change and offer practices to develop the skills to implement change successfully.

Harvard Business Review. **(2011).** *HBR's 10 Must Reads on Change.* **Boston, MA: Harvard Business Publishing.**

These articles will inspire you to lead change through critical stages, establish a sense of urgency, mobilize commitment, diminish the pain of change, and get out of your comfort zone.

Heath, C., & Heath, D. (2010). *Switch: How to Change Things When Change Is Hard.* **New York, NY: Crown Business.**

Change brings on a disjunction between our rational mind and our emotional mind. The rational mind wants to change something at work; the emotional mind loves things as they are. In a story-driven narrative, the authors demonstrate how engaging our emotions and reason can lead to successful change.

Kotter, J. P., & Rathgeber, H. (2006). *Our Iceberg Is Melting: Changing and Succeeding Under Any Conditions.* **New York, NY: St. Martin's Press.**

All too often, people and organizations don't see the need for change. However, change is necessary in this constant shifting business environment. This book uses a simple business management fable to communicate the necessity of change and the challenges of leading change.

Stevenson, J., & Kaafarani, B. (2011). *Breaking Away: How Great Leaders Create Innovation That Drives Sustainable Growth—And Why Others Fail.* **New York, NY: McGraw-Hill.** This book provides a framework to become a business leader with vision who can shape corporate culture to feed innovation. The authors profile best-in-class, innovative organizations and what their leaders do to make innovation a competitive advantage.

Yunus, M. (2003). *Banker to the Poor: Micro-Lending and the Battle Against World Poverty* **(Rev. ed.). Philadelphia, PA: PublicAffairs.** Yunus recounts what led him to fundamentally rethink the economic relationship between rich and poor and the challenges he and his colleagues faced in founding the Grameen Bank. The book traces the origin of microcredit and provides new context on economics, public policy, philanthropy, social history, and business.

"One day our grandchildren will go to museums to see what poverty was like."

– Muhammad Yunus

The degree to which
an individual is motivated by
challenge and can deliver results
in first-time and/or tough
situations through resourcefulness
and by inspiring others

Results
Agility

"You cannot keep determined people from success. If you place stumbling blocks in their way, they will use them for stepping-stones and climb to new heights."

Mary Kay Ash – American entrepreneur

Is the Road to Success
Ever an Easy One?

Mary Kay Ash. Award-winning, phenomenally successful businesswoman whose company thrives in dozens of countries on five continents. In the 21st century, the concept of a woman building a multibillion-dollar business seems almost commonplace. But when Ash embarked on her ambitious journey in 1963, the road was anything but easy. What drove her to take on such a tough challenge? What was it about her that made her beloved by so many? And helped make her two million independent sales agents so successful in their own right?

After watching one too many men whom she had trained get promoted over her, Ash left a successful direct-selling career. Restless, she decided to write a book on the qualities of a dream company that could provide women like her with opportunities. She evaluated and analyzed—what were the positives of her work up to that point? What hindered her career? Though she knew it wouldn't be easy, Ash decided to take her book concept and turn it into an actual business plan that became Mary Kay® cosmetics.

Putting a twist on her direct-selling knowledge, Ash created a business model that put the power and autonomy directly in the hands of her female sales consultants. She knew that starting a business was risky—both for her and for her consultants. In Ash's view, her consultants greatly improved their odds by applying, as she put it, "hard work and tenacity." Ash believed that the road to success is paved with lots of attempts and some failures. To her, it was important to keep learning from them and to keep trying.

Ash's ability to inspire people on a grand scale is well known—from formal speeches at leadership conferences to her foundation work. But it was as much the content of her messages as her overall presence that won Ash such high praise. She focused her messages directly on the needs of her consultants—women who were balancing work and family and who shared her drive to succeed. To this day, many workstations around Mary Kay® headquarters include framed candid photos of Ash with her team members—a testament to her ability to make personal connections.

In many ways, Mary Kay Ash exemplifies Results Agility. She embraced the challenge of creating a company by a woman for women at a time when that was anything but the norm. Through resourcefulness, determination, and the ability to inspire, motivate, and empower others, Ash succeeded in realizing her goal of making life more beautiful for women.

Why Results Agility Matters

Gets results. Drives for results. Results oriented. These descriptors and others like them are probably ones you've heard often before, especially in work settings. All these descriptors also apply when we think about Results Agility. But what *isn't* readily apparent in these phrases is what forms the foundation of Results Agility. Sure, the outcome matters, but the way the results agile person goes about achieving the outcome is what distinguishes them and allows them to have multiple successes across many diverse challenges.

Results Agility is not about doing more of the same. It's about taking on the new, the complex, the difficult. And not just taking it on, but relishing the prospect. When you are results agile, you're energized by challenge—the harder, the better. This doesn't mean being reckless. But it does mean being invigorated by the stretch that the new and different challenge or assignment affords you. And having a stiff spine when the inevitable setbacks come your way.

Many times, the results agile person leaves others scratching their heads, asking, "How'd they do that?" Pulling rabbits out of hats is the calling card of the results agile person. Securing scant resources, fostering support from surly stakeholders, turning failed attempts into learning fodder for the next try—all speak to a resourcefulness that comes with Results Agility.

It's a rare thing today to be able to accomplish anything of significance without the involvement, even commitment, of others. Getting things done through others is key to success in tough assignments. Results Agility is as much about the influence and impact you have on others as it is about your own accomplishments. Setting goals. Delegating. Measuring. Helping. Correcting. Celebrating. That's the cycle of inspiration. And this, coupled with a resourcefulness and resilience when tackling a challenge others might avoid, shows why those with Results Agility are able to make it happen consistently and, often, against the odds.

If you are on the higher end of the Results Agility continuum

You are likely to...

Get the most out of limited resources

Have a strong personal drive to achieve things

Adapt quickly to obstacles and changing circumstances

Instill confidence in others

Be resilient when faced with bad news

Not give up easily

Figure out how to get things done in new and tough situations

Enjoy working on a lot of things at once

And you may say things like...

"I find that I'm more
productive when I have a hundred
things coming at me than when
I have one or two..."

"Yes, it'll be tough, but if
we all keep our eyes on the
prize, I know we can do it..."

"What resources
do we need to make
this happen...?"

If you demonstrate
Results Agility less often

You may...

Pride yourself on doing what is expected of you

Prefer not to be in the spotlight

Respond best when the course of action is clear and predictable

Focus on and like to accomplish tasks one by one

Start with easier tasks before moving on to more difficult ones

Make it a point to get it right the first time

Get discouraged when things don't go as planned

Prefer to get things done by yourself

And you may say things like...

"It's nice to be working
on stuff that's familiar..."

"I like being in the
background more than
being out front..."

"Now this
I can handle...!"

Now you know a little more about Results Agility. Is it about achieving great results? Definitely. But not everyday, run-of-the-mill results. Results that come from new, tough, complex challenges. Challenges that test you and the team you gather to make it happen.

We know that Results Agility is a set of skills and attitudes that can be developed. The next section in this chapter focuses on how you can sharpen your Results Agility. So if you're wondering what it takes to increase Results Agility, demonstrate it more, or make sure you don't overuse it, read on.

Sharpening
your
Results Agility

What Can Sometimes Get in the Way of Demonstrating Results Agility

Before exploring ways to sharpen your Results Agility, it's helpful to think about what may cause you to demonstrate less of this particular agility on a regular basis. Check the causes here that might apply to you. Think about what it looks like and how it may play out in certain situations. And remember that all of these can be addressed if you are motivated to do so.

What might apply to you...

More of an observer than an action-taker

Prefer to follow rather than lead

Like to do things alone

Focus on what is readily attainable

Put off the tough stuff

Uncomfortable with rejection

Value consistency

Take things personally

Significantly value leisure over work activities

Believe there is always one best course of action

Ways to Sharpen Your Results Agility...
Welcome Challenges

Take more risks

Research indicates that successful people have made more mistakes than the less successful. You can't learn anything if you're not trying anything new. Go for small wins so you can recover quickly if you miss the mark and, more importantly, learn from the results. Start with the easiest challenge and then work up to the tougher ones. Like taking on a tough assignment. Many people turn down opportunities based upon current life comforts only to regret it later when they are passed over. Think of that scary and unappealing new task, assignment, or job as an opportunity to add new skills and variety to your experience resume.

Learn on the fly   First-time and tough situations call for resourcefulness. First time means you haven't done exactly this before. We're all pretty good at solving problems we've seen before. When you take on a new, unfamiliar challenge, it means trying solutions you've never tried before. So avoid your own personal favorite solutions at first. Instead, define what it is that needs to be done. Analyze the challenge you're tackling in a new context and in new ways. And be patient. Studies have shown that, on average, the best way forward comes from the second or third solution generated, not the first.

Persevere   When you try something new, something tough, something that others may have found undoable, obstacles and setbacks are almost certain. Sticking to the objective, especially in the face of pushback, is what perseverance is all about. It's also about using a variety of ways to get things done. Persevering people try it different ways when the first way isn't effective. If your first attempt fails, do something totally different next time. Have five different ways to get the same outcome. Be prepared to do them all when obstacles arise.

Ways to Sharpen Your Results Agility...
Be Inspiring

**Build a
common
mind-set**

Nothing galvanizes people like a shared purpose, the glue that holds any group together. Get people involved and rally them around a common vision. Imagine what the outcome will look like if fully realized, then describe it often. Repeatedly sell the logic of pulling together by listening, asking questions, and inviting suggestions to reach the outcome. Leave how things are to be done as open as possible. Keep your focus on the end in mind and others will do the same.

Enhance your presence

If you want people to rally behind you, you have to look and sound like a leader. Project a strong voice. Maintain consistent eye contact. Let others feel your passion, your enthusiasm for meeting challenges. Leading any effort means being on stage, formally or not. All eyes are on you. What impression is formed by the way you carry yourself? By your confidence? You not only deliver a message, you are part of the message. To get others on board to help with a tough assignment, you need to market yourself as someone others should listen to.

Play the motivation odds

Think of three meaningful, personal accomplishments you're proud of, then ask yourself how motivated you were to accomplish them. Similarly, consider what motivates others. Recognize and address the differences in how others are motivated, but understand also that there are similarities. Research shows there are a lot of common underlying motivators that you can apply broadly. When you provide challenges, paint pictures of why achieving the goal is worthwhile, set up chances to learn and grow, and provide autonomy, you'll hit the vast majority of people's motivators.

Ways to Sharpen Your Results Agility...
Execute, Execute, Execute

Plan for the planned and the unplanned

To front-load your chances of success on a tough assignment, start out with a plan. What do you need to accomplish? What's the time line? What resources will you need? Who controls those resources you need—people, funding, tools, materials, support? Lay out the work from A to Z of what you can expect. But be ready for the unexpected. Run scenarios in your head. Think along several paths. Rank the potential problems from highest likelihood to lowest likelihood. Think about what you would do if the highest-likelihood things were to occur. Create a contingency plan for each.

Practice quid pro quo to secure resources

When you need to go outside your own area to reach your goals, influencing skills matter. Don't just ask for things; find some common ground where you can provide help. Are your results important to them? How does what you're working on affect their results? Go into resourcing discussions with a trading mentality. To be seen as more cooperative, always explain your thinking and invite them to explain theirs. Generate lots of possibilities before staking out positions. Allow them room to talk it through from their perspectives. Focus on common goals, priorities, and problems.

Unleash the power of delegation

With big, complex, challenging assignments, it's highly unlikely you can do it all yourself. Getting results through others means delegating effectively. To do it well, you need to set clear priorities, time frames, goals, then get out of the way. Keep lines of communication open and provide help when needed. On the front end, be very clear on the *what* and *when*, but be very open on the *how*. People are more motivated when they can determine the how themselves. Encourage them to try things. Delegate complete tasks, not pieces.

Be Mindful Not to Overuse Results Agility

Too much of most anything isn't necessarily a good thing. The same holds true for Results Agility.

While there is much about being results agile that is helpful, flexing this agility indiscriminately may hurt group process or cause issues with relationships. Left unchecked, overusing Results Agility could minimize or erase its benefits altogether.

People who overuse their Results Agility may...

Take on challenges that far exceed their or their team's capabilities

Become involved in too many things at once; overcommit

Push solutions before adequate analysis

Get results at all costs without appropriate concern for people, teams, due process or, possibly, organizational norms and ethics

Stubbornly continue efforts in the face of overwhelming evidence to the contrary

As you focus on building Results Agility, temper potential overuse in these ways...

Become adept at prioritizing so you don't spread yourself (and your team) too thin

Weigh the evidence and get comfortable knowing when it's time to call it quits on a doomed project

Balance your can-do attitude with a healthy dose of "is it really doable?" questioning before committing resources

Slow down a little before diving into a new opportunity; get clear on what problem you're trying to solve by taking on the assignment

Consider the upstream, downstream, and sidestream consequences of your actions; avoid a rigid ends-justify-the-means mentality

For more help balancing possible Results Agility overuse, read "Think It Through" in the Mental Agility chapter, and "Be a Feedback Seeker" in the Self-Awareness chapter.

Assignments to Build and Reinforce Results Agility

On the Job

Chair a project or task force requiring you to craft a new solution under tight deadlines and with high visibility. This will help you practice contingency planning and how to find and use resources quickly.

Take on a fix-it or turnaround assignment where you will need to make tough decisions impacting a variety of people and constituencies in a challenging environment. Here you will need to focus on the outcome or future-state which will motivate people to overcome any hurdles that may emerge along the way.

Begin something new from scratch which will require you to form a new team and initiate a number of simultaneous actions under a tight time frame. You will likely need to practice resilience for the unexpected and possibly unpleasant that comes with any new venture.

On or Off the Job

Manage a group of inexperienced people as their coach, teacher, guide, or mentor. This will give you practice inspiring others.

Assemble a team of diverse people to accomplish a difficult task where you can't go it alone and others are integral to success. Tap into their motivation triggers to help them (and the group's objective) be successful.

Take on a task you dislike or even hate doing to build up your going-against-the-grain experiences.

Read More About Results Agility

Adair, J. (2009). *The Inspirational Leader: How to Motivate, Encourage, and Achieve Success* (Reissue ed.). Philadelphia, PA: Kogan Page.

Taking the form of conversations between a young chief executive and the author, *The Inspirational Leader* explores the nature and practice of leadership, and each aspect is studied and discussed so that the key skills are revealed for anyone to adopt and use to inspire and encourage others.

Ash, M. K. (2008). *The Mary Kay Way: Timeless Principles from America's Greatest Woman Entrepreneur* (Updated ed.). Hoboken, NJ: John Wiley & Sons.

This book includes the inspiration and success principles of Mary Kay Ash, the founder of Mary Kay Inc., the cosmetics company that helps women have their own businesses.

Burnison, G. (2011). *No Fear of Failure: Real Stories of How Leaders Deal with Risk and Change.* San Francisco, CA: Jossey-Bass.

This book offers insightful, candid conversations with top leaders in business, politics, education, and philanthropy, with first-person accounts of how they approached crucial, career-defining moments. These leaders show the risks one must be willing to take, and the vision, resilience, and compassion necessary to lead.

Leary-Joyce, J. (2011). *Inspirational Manager: How to Build Relationships That Deliver Results* (2nd ed.). Upper Saddle River, NJ: FT Press.

Drawing on the experiences of real inspirational managers, *Inspirational Manager* provides useful strategies and action plans for achieving success across various management disciplines. It includes helpful ways for you to engage with your staff, deal with difficult situations, and deliver results.

Lepsinger, R. (2010). *Closing the Execution Gap: How Great Leaders and Their Companies Get Results.* **San Francisco, CA: Jossey-Bass.**

Successful organizations are successful because they are able to execute their strategies by (1) creating and using action plans, (2) expecting and getting top performance, (3) holding people accountable, (4) involving the right people in the right decisions, (5) facilitating change readiness, and (6) enhancing cooperation and collaboration.

"There are four kinds of people in this world:

- those who make things happen
- those who watch things happen
- those who wonder what happened
- those who don't know that anything happened!

I knew from a very early age that
I wanted to be first on that list."

– Mary Kay Ash

Afterword

Self-Awareness – Gaining personal insights for a purpose

Mental Agility – Curiosity with a penchant for creatively solving complex problems

People Agility – Knowing, reading, valuing, and adapting to others

Change Agility – Posing the questions that get us to look at things differently

Results Agility – Getting things done against the odds

Much has been explored in these chapters on Learning Agility and the five agility factors. Hopefully you've uncovered some insights into how you or people you know may demonstrate some of the agility behaviors described here.

As you venture forth, armed with a better understanding of Learning Agility and how it can help you navigate an increasingly complex and uncertain world, here are some things to consider doing next:

Get the Most Out of Your Experiences

Having a high degree of Learning Agility is very beneficial for leadership roles. It is also helpful in many, but not all, other situations.

First, think about your past and current job or roles:

> Have they provided you with a fertile ground of diverse experiences from which you can harvest meaning and then convert that meaning into lessons you can use in the future?

> Or, have the roles helped you deepen and hone your current skills by providing increasing degrees of challenge within your area of expertise?

Next, given where you've been and where you are now, forecast into the future:

> Where do you see the path of your career headed? And does that measure up with what you *want* to see?

If you aspire to broad leadership roles or opportunities that will offer an ample supply of new and diverse challenges, then building up your Learning Agility will be an important step in enabling you to achieve that objective.

If you aspire to be a deep expert in an area you are passionate about, then continuously adding the skills that build on your mastery will help you with that goal.

Get a Pulse on Your Level of Self-Awareness

Regardless of the path you are on and the one you aspire to, the one Learning Agility factor that stands out as a common benefit to all is Self-Awareness. Without an understanding of your strengths and weaknesses, it will be difficult to anticipate where the land mines are in those new challenges, whether unfamiliar and diverse or expertise building.

You can do this right away, either formally or informally. Informally, start asking people around you to vet your assumptions about how you come across—remember to include people who may not be your biggest fans. Formally, find an assessment where you can gauge how accurate your own perception is when it comes to your current skills.

Take Time to Reflect

The fastest way to start building your Self-Awareness is through reflection. So make reflecting a habit. Reflect on anything that strikes you—people interactions, decision fallout, wins, losses, and so on. Find ways to jot down your personal "ahas" as close to when they happen as possible. You can then start vetting those ahas with others.

So now it's up to you:

Know what you want out of your career

Build the skills and agility that will get you there

Reflect throughout

And, above all, keep learning.

Acknowledgments

A number of people contributed to the creation of this book and deserve a great deal of thanks and appreciation.

This book would not be possible without Bob Eichinger and Mike Lombardo. Their rich legacy of research and intellectual property on Learning Agility is the bedrock upon which this book is built. Many of this book's development tips are derived from their work.

Thanks to Guangrong Dai, Ken De Meuse, George Hallenbeck, Erica Lutrick, and Evelyn Orr for their thought partnership and suggestions for the book chapters and for contributing such rich examples for the Learning Agility factor portraits. Special thanks to King Yii (Lulu) Tang for providing helpful descriptions for the suggested readings in each chapter.

A special appreciation for the thoughtful review and insights provided by Bob Eichinger, Zoe Hruby, Kara Kelly, Dana Landis, Jim Peters, Stacy Rider, Linda Rodman, and Kim Ruyle.

The translation of this book into several different languages would not have been possible without the tireless contributions of Valérie Petit.

Thanks to the core team of Phil Boehlke, Eric Ekstrand, Diane Hoffmann Kotila, Lesley Kurke, Doug Lodermeier, Bonnie Parks, and La Tasha Reed for their hard work and dedication.

Notes

Introduction

1. United Nations Department of Economic and Social Affairs. (2006). *World population prospects: The 2004 revision.* New York, NY: United Nations Publishing.

2. The Conference Board. (2011). *The 2011 CEO Succession Report.* New York, NY: Author.

3. Bunker, K., Kram, K., & Ting, S. (2002, December). The young and the clueless: How to manage your bad boys. *Harvard Business Review, 80*(12).

4. Hall, D. T. (2004). Self-awareness, identity, and leader development. In D. V. Day, S. J. Zaccaro, & S. M. Halpin (Eds.), *Leader development for transforming organizations: Growing leaders for tomorrow* (pp. 153–176). Mahwah, NJ: Lawrence Erlbaum Associates.

Learning Agility Unveiled

5. Branson, R. (2006). *Screw it, let's do it: Lessons in life.* London: Virgin Books Ltd.

6. Branson, R. (2010, November). *60 Questions for my 60th year.* Retrieved November 9, 2011, from http://www.virgin.com/richard-branson/blog/

7. Finkelstein, S. (2010). *No more bad decisions.* New Word City, Inc. Available from http://www.newwordcity.com/books/all/no-more-bad-decisions

8. McCall, M. W., Jr., Lombardo, M. M., & Morrison, A. (1988). *The lessons of experience.* New York, NY: Free Press.

9. Goldsmith, M. (2007). *What got you here won't get you there.* New York, NY: Hyperion.

10. Lombardo, M. M., & Eichinger, R. W. (2000). High potentials as high learners. *Human Resource Management, 39*(4), 321–330.

11. Lombardo, M. M., & Eichinger, R. W. (2011). *The leadership machine* (10th Anniversary ed.). Minneapolis, MN: Lominger International: A Korn/Ferry Company.

12. Sternberg, R. J. (1985). *Beyond IQ: A triarchic theory of intelligence.* New York, NY: Cambridge University Press.

13. Pink, D. (2006). *A whole new mind: Why right-brainers will rule the future.* New York: Penguin Group.

14. McCauley, C. D., Ruderman, M. N., Ohlott, P. J., & Morrow, J. E. (1994). Assessing the developmental components of managerial jobs. *Journal of Applied Psychology, 79*(4), 544–560.

15. De Meuse, K. P. (2008). Learning agility: A new construct whose time has come. In R. B. Kaiser (Chair), *The importance, assessment, and development of flexible leadership*. Symposium presented at the annual conference for the Society for Industrial and Organizational Psychology, San Francisco, CA.

16. Lominger International. (2010). *Choices Architect® technical manual* (2nd ed.). Minneapolis, MN: Lominger International: A Korn/Ferry Company.

17. De Meuse, K., Dai, G., Eichinger, R., Page, R., Clark, L., & Zewdie, S. (2011) *The development and validation of a self assessment of learning agility* [Technical Report]. Los Angeles, CA: The Korn/Ferry Institute.

18. Altman, A. (2009, January 16). *Chesley B. Sullenberger III.* [2-Min Bio]. Retrieved November 9, 2011, from http://www.time.com/time/nation article/0,8599,1872247,00.html

19. Gladwell, M. (2008). *Outliers: The story of success.* New York, NY: Little, Brown & Company.

References

Self-Awareness

Angelou, M. (1981). *The heart of a woman.* New York, NY: Modern Library.

Gillespie, M., Butler, R., & Long, R. (2008). *Maya Angelou: A glorious celebration.* New York, NY: Doubleday.

Harper, J. (2010). *Maya Angelou.* Mankato, MN: Child's World.

Kite, L. P. (1999). *Maya Angelou.* Minneapolis, MN: Lerner Publications.

Winfrey, O. (2000, December). Oprah talks to Maya Angelou. [Interview]. *O, The Oprah Magazine.* Retrieved November 9, 2011, from http://www.oprah.com/omagazine/Oprah-Interviews-Maya-Angelou/10#ixzz1bnXlwTqa

Mental Agility

PBS Home Video Series. (2006, August 16). Albert Einstein: How I see the world (Part 1 of 6). *American Masters* [Television series]. Retrieved January 10, 2012, from http://www.pbs.org/wnet/americanmasters/episodes/albert-einstein/how-i-see-the-world/585/ Video retrieved September 30, 2011, from http://www.youtube.com/watch?v=RVJyaJ5TNpc

People Agility

Stengel, R. (2009). *Mandela's way: Fifteen lessons on life, love, and courage.* New York, NY: Crown Publishing.

Change Agility

A short history of Grameen Bank. (n.d.). Retrieved November 4, 2011, from http://www.grameen-info.org/index.php?option=com_content&task=view&id=19&Itemid=114

Robert F. Kennedy Center for Justice & Human Rights. (2010). *Speak truth to power: Muhammad Yunus.* Retrieved January 10, 2012, from http://blogs.nysut.org/sttp/defenders/muhammad-yunus/

Yunus, M. (2003). *Banker to the poor: Micro-lending and the battle against world poverty* (Rev. ed.). Philadelphia, PA: Public Affairs.

Results Agility

Ash, M. K. (2008). *The Mary Kay way: Timeless principles from America's greatest woman entrepreneur* (Updated ed.). Hoboken, NJ: John Wiley & Sons.

Celebrating Mary Kay Ash. (n.d.). Retrieved November 8, 2011, from http://www.marykaytribute.com/default.aspx

Mary Kay Ash: One of the greatest female entrepreneurs in American history. (n.d.). Retrieved November 18, 2011, from http://www.marykay.com/company/companyfounder/default.aspx

Resources for Individuals

In addition to the tips, recommendations, and suggestions for further reading in the Learning Agility chapters, here are some additional tools that can help you on your journey to explore and potentially build your Learning Agility.

Becoming an Agile Leader App can help you achieve greater self-awareness through capturing on-the-spot insights and reflections. *Becoming an Agile Leader* App provides inspiring, thought-provoking quotes related to the Learning Agility factors which will help you easily reflect, document, and transfer learnings from your experiences.

With *Becoming an Agile Leader: A Guide to Learning From Your Experiences,* you can explore the formative experiences that shaped the learning agile leaders profiled in the book *Becoming an Agile Leader.* This practical guide lets you reflect on your own experiences, past and present, and includes a comprehensive listing of on- and off-the-job experiences that will help you plan for assignments that build Learning Agility.

FYI™ for Insight will help you understand 21 leadership characteristics for success and 5 characteristics that can derail your career. It will also make you aware of *why* you may be lacking skill or motivation in certain areas. This is critical because becoming self-aware can get you 50% of the way toward improving your performance.

Insight into strengths and weaknesses can help you get what you want from your career. The *FYI™ for Insight* Self-Awareness Assessment is a three-step process that takes just a few minutes. A personalized report gives you a self-awareness score and highlights your hidden strengths and blind spots.

More information on these resources can be found at http://www.lominger.com

Resources for Organizations

Research has clearly shown that Learning Agility is a primary component and key differentiator of potential for leadership roles. By understanding and leveraging Learning Agility in your organization, you can better distinguish between current performance and future potential and create a more targeted, differentiated development strategy for current and future leaders. The assessment and development tools here can help you integrate Learning Agility into your organization's strategic talent management initiatives.

Assessments

viaEDGE™ easily and efficiently gauges the Learning Agility of large numbers of individuals, with the ease of an online self-administered assessment. viaEDGE™ helps organizations assess internal talent for placement and development of high potentials and can aid in external candidate hiring. *Available in multiple languages.*

Choices Architect® has been used for years by organizations to identify, validate, and select those who are the most learning agile. Choices Architect® scores have been significantly related to independent measures or ratings of potential, consistent performance, and staying out of trouble. This well-validated assessment is available in multiple formats, including an online multi-rater survey. *Available in multiple languages.*

Learning From Experience™ (LFE) Interview Guide is a selection tool designed to assist employers with assessing learning agility in the interviewing process. The guide helps organizations build future bench strength through interviewing and selecting the most learning agile internal and external candidates.

Development Tools

Learning Agility can be developed. *FYI™ for Learning Agility* is designed for any motivated person seeking to develop skills that lead to increased Learning Agility. It includes 200+ improvement and workaround strategies that individuals can use today on or off the job.

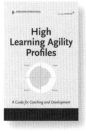

Are all highly learning agile individuals the same? The *High Learning Agility Profiles* guide helps learning agile individuals identify which of the seven distinct profiles best fits them, which situations favor their learning agility strengths, and the best opportunities for further developing their learning agility.

More information on these resources can be found at http://www.lominger.com